On Wings of Song

A Journey into the Civil Rights Era

Also by Molly Lynn Watt

Poetry

Shadow People
Consider This

Play

George & Ruth: Songs & Letters of the Spanish Civil War
Co-authored with Daniel Lynn Watt

Editor

Bagels with the Bards, Numbers 1, 2, 3 & 4

On Wings of Song

A Journey into the Civil Rights Era

for Marilyn,
with gratitude
in admiration
and in friendship.
Molly
9.02.14

Poems

Molly Lynn Watt

Molly Lynn Watt

Cover Painting *Good Company,* by Bridget Galway
Cover Design by Steve Glines and Dan Lynn Watt
Book Design by Steve Glines

First Edition

Library of Congress Cataloging-in-PublicationData

Watt, Molly Lynn, 1938—

ISBN 978-0-9678131-3-4

Ibbetson Street Press
25 School Street
Somerville, Mass

For the
thousands of ordinary citizens
carried on wings of song
during the nonviolent struggle
of the Civil Rights Movement

The things you start may not come to fruition on your timetable. But you can move things forward. And sometimes the things that start out small may turn out to be fairly significant.

Barack Obama, the White House

I am not weaving my life's patterns alone. Only one end of the threads do I hold in my hands. The other ends go many ways linking my life with others.

Septima Clark, Highlander Center

At Highlander Center I learned I had white allies.

Rosa Parks, Montgomery Bus Boycott

I want to write poems
the way a jazz man
composes on his feet
sways in rhythm
taps a syncopated beat

I want to howl and growl
to a bottleneck slide
pulse with rage and heat
rap a wild wind run
to blast away injustice

Instead I strain and stutter
of a young family's journey—
like thousands of others—
in the unfolding drama
of the Civil Rights Movement

CONTENTS

BEFORE 1963

Yes

my people owned slaves
split husband from wife
traded parent from child
worked folks like mules
plowed with sinew and bone
watered fields with sweat
washed cotton with tears
yes
this is the stain
my forebears
passed to me
slaves bought at auction
slaves sold for profit
yes
my people were
slaveholding midwives to the nation
my mother framed and hung
a bill of sale
in the parsonage parlor
like an ongoing lynching
yes
I own my inheritance
yes
I strive for justice
yes

Daddy Takes Me to Meet Abe Lincoln (1946)

on the Washington Mall
a girl steps off the bus
her foot catches in the door
she tumbles to the street
the bus rumbles into motion
drags the child along the gutter
a soldier shakes his fist
howls and chases after—
the gathering crowd begins to shriek

Daddy runs into the street
I tremble by his side
the bus is rolling at us
the driver honks the horn
Daddy stands up tall
holds his hand up like a cop
shouts *stop* *for god's sake stop*
brakes screech the bus halts
the driver calls out *black or white?*
the crowd yells back *dead!*

the bus door releases
the girl slumps to the street
her party dress torn and bloody
the soldier father kneels
tries to soothe his daughter
sirens sweep aside the crowd
medics bear the girl away

Daddy hails a cab
—weeping
we wedge in with the father
chase to the ER
wait for the verdict
she breathes
she will recover

Daddy grasps the soldier's hand
God be with you and your daughter
I brought mine to meet Abe Lincoln
but she met Jim Crow instead

Scrapbook of a Connecticut Schoolgirl (1940s–1950s)

when seven
you walked a mile to and fro to school twice a day
in unsupervised freedom   but for five-year-old
Lynette Kwock   a gauntlet of *yellow-girl* taunts
your mother said *keep ahold of that girl's hand*

when eleven
your friend Sally's mother invited you to tea to meet
a tall Negro woman from Philadelphia   Pennsylvania
Miss Marion Anderson talked of hymns and singing—
songs soar beyond where you are welcome

when twelve
your family moved to the country
your father said *no room on the school bus*
a townsman sent his driver and limo to drive
you and the only black kids in town to school

when fifteen
your father thought you *boy-crazy* and your mother said
academically lazy and packed you off to boarding school
to bunk with a black girl from Tennessee and be taught by someone
who could not speak of living in a camp for Japanese Americans

when eighteen
you chose a college in Maine
one person of color enrolled
you felt so white   so chilled   so desolate
you fled   got yourself hitched

The Boy Almost Next Door (1950s)

his mother says *he's all Yankee*
his father says *half Swedish*
shhh! no one says he's a quarter Indian

Bob didn't consider Gramma Della's skin color—
brown as the horse chestnuts falling in the yard
prickly as the husks by the picket fence

maybe like the Selkie she'd shed her skin on the other side of Lake
Char-gogg-a-gogg-man-chaugg-a-gogg-chau-bun-a-gun-ga-maugg
held out an apple to the horse owned by the whiskey-drinking junkman—

bingo— she had a new life wrapped up in the American dream
Gramps and Gramma Della slept in the rope bed in the attic
close to the music of wind and the dance of mice

Bob was embarrassed by his rumpled Gramps's drinking
and by his dad's Swedish accent   but proud that his dad—
though not required—dressed for work in a suit and tie

Bob's mother never met his dad's folks   didn't allow Swedish
but on Christmas Eve   she let his dad take him to *farmor's*
to drink boiled coffee inside the swirling sound of Swedish

Bob jumped the broom with the minister's daughter
packed off for the city
never looked back

Billie Holiday Sings "Strange Fruit" (1958)

in a Connecticut nightclub
a woman enters
through eddies of cigarette smoke
a gardenia behind her ear
her white satin gown
too loose for her frame
unsteady   she leans on an escort
makes her way to the stage
her ringed hands limp at her waist
she stares through the crowd
opens her ruby mouth
a low dry voice drips
flooding the room
southern trees bear a strange fruit

Billie   head high   eyes shut
puts Jim Crow on stage
I am a witness under the live oak
I am the lynching party
I am the body swaying on the rope
I am not breathing
Lady Day burns out note after note
scorching the darkness
here is a strange and a bitter crop

Lady sways a little
her escort helps her from the stage
someone   claps
another joins
the room applauds
as Lady Day fades away

I am twenty
witnessing
a double lynching—
the body hanging in the song
the singer ravaged by drugs—
later
under the attic eaves
in Gramps and Della's rope bed
bone-chilled   I
can't get warm enough
can't get close enough
Bob and I conceive our first child
to a chorus of howling ghosts

Happily Ever After? (1962)

a mummy Molly
a daddy Bob
three-year-old Robin with eyes like sky
one-year-old Kristin with eyes like earth
a two-bedroom Cambridge apartment
a postage-stamp yard

like his dad Bob wears a tie to his 9-to-5 job
like her mum Molly wears an apron
keeps everything humming

the kids tickle and giggle
mew like cats roar like lions
splash like fish in the bath
Bob chain-smokes in rhythm
Molly sighs through the day
though nothing is wrong

they support peace and rights
stuff envelopes at night
all is harmonious no pandemonium
they are bored
want something big
seek something more

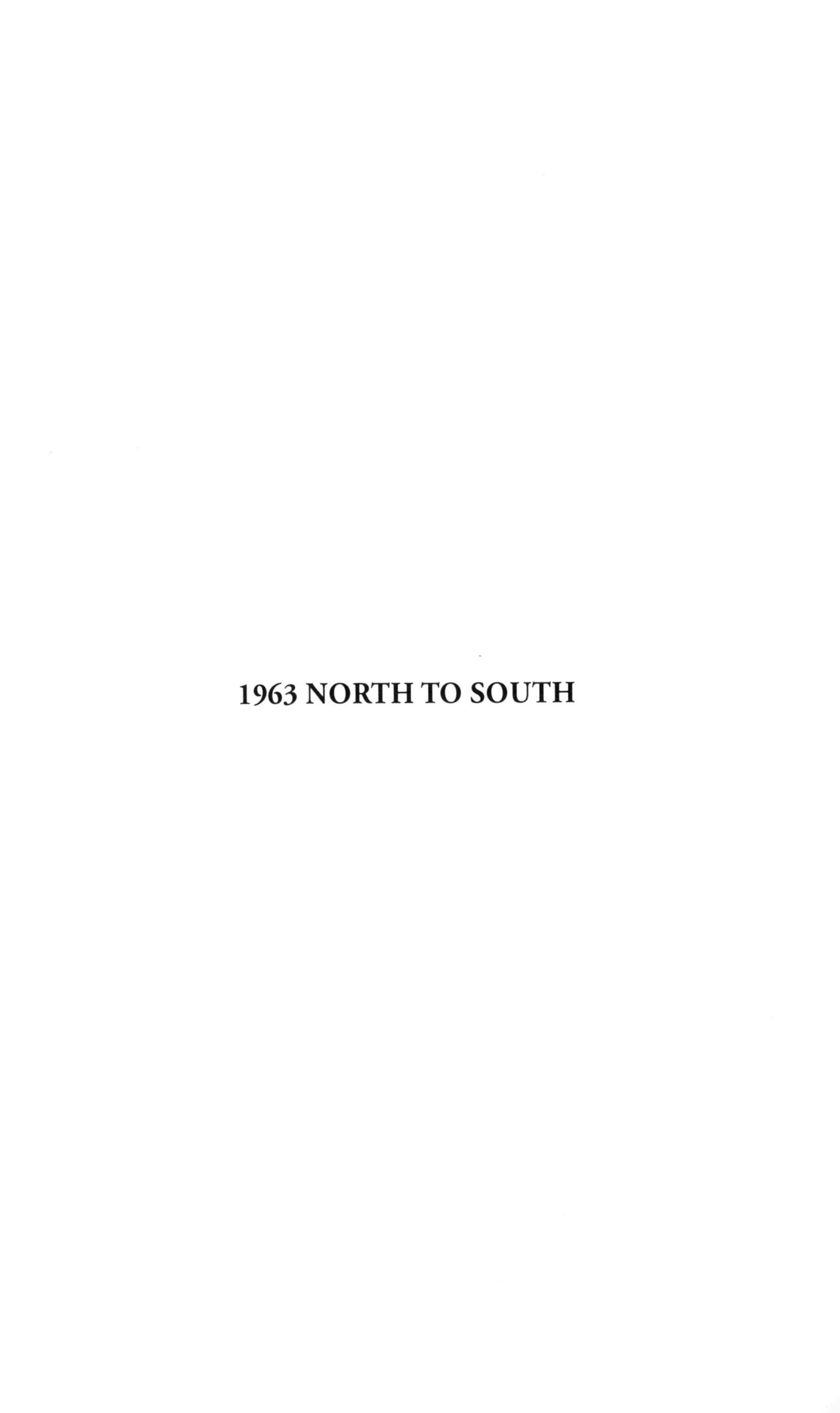

1963 NORTH TO SOUTH

New Year's Day

weather advisories
blizzard conditions
highway paralysis
the plucky family sets forth
in a Volkswagen bug
three car payments to go
two graduate school loans
four suitcases
four sleeping bags
one box of cheerios
a six-string guitar
The Feminine Mystique
plus two bottles of pink medicine
for the kids' ear infections

this was her
home-sweet-home getaway

In the Communal Kitchen in Putney, Vermont

Bob mixes a batter for honey bread
Jean squeezes lime on his Haitian rice dish
Morris tells the kids a Brer Rabbit tale
Molly strains to hear over the wishy-washy

Morris declares *the end* chants
Molly want Brer Rabbit's carrot?
what? Molly couldn't hear my story?
you say the wall's in the way?

Morris hauls out a sledgehammer
whacks the wall until it crumbles
into a heap of rubble proclaims
a wall in the way take it down!

we chose Morris Mitchell
he directs the Putney Graduate School
we won't bog down in textbooks
nor stick in statistics we'll know action

East Harlem

we drive 200 miles to New York City
to study what some call *the Puerto Rican Problem*
in what others call *the trash heap of America*

people are staring
at us?
are we staring back?

through reeking urine decaying food
we enter candlelight a community meal
banter in Spanish joshing in English

word arrives
the mirror on our car smashed
our knapsacks vamoosed

in the gleaming maze
of this Friends Neighborhood House
I've lost sight of three-year-old Robin

Johnny Torres a gang leader *gone social*
piggybacks Robin onto my lap
both laughing

Miguel helps me settle the kids for bed
pulls out a snapshot of a black man
handsome smiling holding a child

I like kids but don't trap me like my sister
that's her Nelson serving time—
no more dope no more rumbles for me

but no job either   I dropped out of school
I'm no Johnny Torres—can't make up Al Capone plays
nothing for me here   I'm headed back to Puerto Rico

the waft of marijuana precedes Manuel
he shoves knapsacks across the floor
guess they found their way back from the street!

Three Vermont Schools

we drop the kids at preschool
in a made-over chicken coop
here they can paint on anything
pour maple syrup on snow
and eat it

Bob's internship in high school
gets him wrestling chairs
intercepting love notes
ducking spitballs
while discussing *Walden*

on the first day I take on third grade
I watch a student lead
the pledge of allegiance *to God*
pray to *the American flag*
all nine-year-olds recite   no one blinks

That April

That April when the children marched in Birmingham
a loaf of Wonder Bread cost a quarter
a jar of Skippy peanut butter cost three
you could fill a VW gas tank for two fifty

That April when the children marched in Birmingham
we folded our lives into a Volkswagen bug
took off south with an international, interracial caravan
to see what democracy can do by studying the TVA

That April when the children marched in Birmingham
the Easter Bunny hopped over the Holyoke Mountain Range
down the Hudson River Valley   across the Blue Ridge Mountains
900 miles to drop Easter baskets for our girls

That April when the children marched in Birmingham
the Kennedys held an egg hunt in the Rose Garden
our group finished a brunch of Aunt Jemima pancakes
payback   the Ku Klux Klan firebombed the café

That April when the children marched in Birmingham
Bull Connor ordered fire hoses aimed at protesters
the news coverage stunned the world
jets rip shirts off boys   police dogs attack kids

That April when the children marched in Birmingham
the Red Sox beat the Senators three to nothing in DC
Rev. King wrote on scraps from jail imploring unity
a truck aimed for our VW   bumped us into a ditch

Road Signs

welcome to Tennessee
the volunteer state

the hog and hominy state
the big bend state

dim your lights / behind a car
let folks see / how bright you are / Burma Shave

drinking fountain for whites only
coloreds fountain in the rear

whites seated at the counter
coloreds takeout at the rear

Dinah doesn't / treat him right
if he'd shave / dyna-mite / Burma Shave

whites restroom enter here
coloreds restroom in the rear

whites line up at bus front
coloreds enter at bus rear

whites only beyond this point
no dogs   no negroes   Jim Crow lives here

the monkey took / one look at Jim
and threw the peanuts / back at him / Burma Shave

Tennessee Valley Authority—Showpiece for Democracy

1
from Morris I heard:

we'll whiz down interstates   mosey up and down dirt roads
walk on and under dams   in and out of power plants
talk to folks in schools   hospitals   courts   commerce
visit in homes   listen to stories   sing their songs
I'll forge grooves in your brains deep enough to hold this big idea:

reconstruction can better the lives of ordinary people

(raised in these parts   Morris was sure
my mother   from hereabouts   always skeptical)

2
from my mother I knew:

these parts are home
to good people   but weary
wrestling worn-out soil
raising corn for livestock
tobacco   for a cash crop
growing up younguns who will
move on to the city for wages

when hard times hit
like when the Depression slammed 'em
many hitched back to the mountains
built a cabin   planted crops
raised up a batch of kids
didn't need fancy roads   no cars
didn't need trucks   drove mules
didn't need fancy schools   got by on basics
didn't need doctors   neighbor nursed neighbor
didn't need indoor plumbing   used out-yonder

didn't need running water   bathed in the creek
they made about everything they needed
singing work along the way my mother sang us
as we snapped beans and washed up dishes
on our patch of farm in Connecticut

(my mother got out on a full scholarship to Vassar—
but she was always dirt-poor   always independent)

3
from my father's stories I learned:

the President sat in his wheelchair
contemplating stacks of photographs
like ones in your mother's scrapbook
patched-up houses on patches of dirt
a man plowing behind a mule
a woman doing wash in a galvanized tub
kids walking barefoot to a bare school
countryside blowing away
looked kind of picturesque
but FDR wasn't fooled
he knew the numbers
America could do better
he had a deal for every American—
a home with indoor plumbing
an electric stove and fridge
no more slavery in the kitchen for women
and he'd put men to work harnessing the river

(my father   a country clergyman
put his faith in FDR)

4

from Pete Seeger I understood:

in 1933
this guy from DC
calling himself Uncle Sam
strode into this valley
in a billow of dust
to improve the lot of common folk
told 'em *we're putting up a dam*
to power the community
make it hum on e-lec-tri-ci-ty
this was the New Deal to save America
he flooded over the land
tilled for generations by mountain people
raised a mountain of concrete
spanning the Clinch River
for most of the mountain people
their improved lot meant
moving further up the mountain
—still dirt poor—
starting all over from scratch

(maybe that's when mountain people
made up their minds they didn't want outsiders
coming in and telling them their business
no matter where my mother lived she claimed
all politicians are liars!)

I Spy

our bug burns up the highway
tailgates tractor-trailer trucks
whizzes through Alabama

the kids dive into the boot
slide down the seat   roll
on the floor   I say *I spy*

starting with mmm
Robin pops up *that man!*
Kristin points *doggy!*

a tall man pushes a postal cart
down US Highway 11
a tagalong mongrel for company

Robin shouts *I spy something with sss*
the hand-lettered sign on his back
reads *end segregation*

a white man on a dangerous mission
Bob U-turns to cheer this fellow on
but the man is limping barefoot up a knoll

next day's radio news   *integrationist dead*
two shots to head   mutt guards body
probably someone just passing through

(years later I will learn it was William Lewis Moore—
April 28, 1927–April 23, 1963—a Baltimore postman
walking to petition Governor Barnett to end segregation)

Fayette County, Tennessee

1

our caravan switches roads like switching channels
but everything is in black *or* white
run-down homes   worn-off white paint
black farmers plow black earth with dark mules
late spring cotton planting
feels like summer   our group is parched
but signs say *whites only* or *coloreds only*
my little family of four looks white   but
our group is international *and integrated—*
from Haiti   Jamaica   India   West Indies
New Jersey   Massachusetts   Vermont

2

a sign outside Somerville
McFerren's Groceries and Oil
no color stipulation
the owner John McFerren appears
in overalls   grins   he's black
pumps gas   *always be ready to leave!*
takes orders for ice cream   for coke
proud of his gut and sweat miracle
John McFerren unwinds his story
I took over this store when my brother quit
I supply what Negroes need
we can only improve our lot with the vote
but anyone trying to register is fired and evicted—
no one will sell to Negroes for credit or cash
I'm blacklisted at warehouses
spend my nights driving back roads
getting stuff from black store owners—
see that '53 Ford   got a Thunderbird motor
four-barreled carburetors   does 135 an hour
can outrun the White Citizens Council
can outrun the Klan

3

we switch channels again
destination: the Somerville Courthouse
purpose: to interview employees
to learn about voter registration
only white males seem to work here
no one's in a hurry   we sit
we wait   we wait   we wait
Bob goes for a smoke
I hold baby Kristin
Jean   our Haitian colleague
lifts my three-year-old onto his lap
the clerk looks at golden-haired Robin
at Jean's black arms holding her
the clerk tells me   *little lady   come back*
when you can leave your babies at home
and don't bring your hired man again either!

4

our international caravan of students
weary of threats   of epithet-slingers   of attackers   of stalkers
of laboring to find food service   shelter   bathrooms   a drink of water
guns the engines
to where blacks and whites are welcome   together

Highlander Folk School

a school for folk
a school for ordinary folk
folk working for bread and butter
for bread and butter and humanity
for bread and butter and justice
folks for justice
justice for all citizens
a school for citizens
for citizenship training
for common folk to attend
Highlander Folk School founded in 1932—
same year the TVA took over these parts—
has no chalkboard or desks   just
a round table
some rocking chairs
some books
a few big ideas—
ideas slide inside heads
worm into hearts
pop out of mouths
transform into actions

(oh   that explains
why singing freedom songs make you a communist
why billboards discredit Dr. King for attending
this alleged *Communist Training Camp)*

Myles Horton

sits reading at the table
a pot of coffee brewing
hair slicked back   slacks pressed
looking like an ordinary man
he could be my father
in that Connecticut farmhouse
where I was raised
doesn't seem like the so-called
radical hillbilly
beaten up   locked up
railed against   harassed
holding the State of Tennessee hostage
by teaching nonviolent action
fired by participant research

where are the desks
for this Highlander School?
the chalkboards?   the textbooks?
the classrooms?

Myles Horton says—
I like to keep things simple
I love the practical wisdom
of common people
when one has a problem—
say registering voters—
I invite folks to the table
          share what you do
          what you know
          what you need
of course experts come
in all colors and stripes
while talking together
they forget old Jim Crow

Myles stirs his coffee—
of course the South always had
nighttime integration
it's daytime integration
Highlander's promoting—
he chuckles

I feel tall at this table
Bob and I found purpose
come summer
a job full of promise

Side Trip to Mexico

1

our group travels unpaved roads
unmarked streets   eats for pesos
por favor oranges   tortillas
refried beans sun-warm beer
sleeps in dorms at Casa de los Amigos
sleeps on floors in Uruapan Weaving Co-op
sleeps in pastures with cows
sleeps on beaches

we nomads for ideas frequent
cooperative stores
cooperative farming
cooperative banks
cooperative fishing

2

we wrap ourselves in Rivera's murals
history lessons in paint—no literacy needed
the sun   the land   the blood
the peasants   the laborers   the soldiers
the vast erotic current
running through in female form
a mother   with watchful eyes
with immense womb
ripe for revolutionary seed
a world in flux
paradise   germination   procreation
under huge green leaves
Rivera paints the way

3
we talk politics   talk revolution
in English   in Spanish   in French
headlines from home *Dylan grabs buzz*
will not compromise for Ed Sullivan on TV
Haiti smolders in revolution
Birmingham rivets world attention

4
Kristin's first day   *vaca*
Kristin's last day   *naranja*   *pollo*   *niños*
Robin's first day   *kids play the same in Spanish and English*
Robin's last day *why do the clouds walk on the mountains*
singing which side are you on?

Ready or Not!

we slurp the remaining oranges
bid our international cohort adios
cross back into the US
seamlessly
knowing others are being detained
for no apparent reason

we organizers-in-training
are ready to roll up our sleeves
sweat for citizen rights—
Highlander Folk School and Myles Horton
North South Smoky Mountain Workcamp
here we come!

we hit the gas for Tennessee

1963 NORTH SOUTH SMOKY MOUNTAIN WORKCAMP

In 1963

when Commissioner Bull Connor set dogs and hoses on children
marching in the streets of Birmingham

when Reverend King wrote from Birmingham Jail *injustice anywhere is a threat to justice everywhere*

when Governor Wallace stood on the university steps to block two
African Americans from enrolling

when President Kennedy addressed the nation on *a moral issue ... old as the scriptures ... clear as the Constitution*

when Medgar Evers—carrying T-shirts emblazoned with *Jim Crow must go* — took a bullet to his head

when many blamed peaceful demonstrators for provoking the violence

when the world watched the scattershot of nonviolent actions cross the
nation

when the world watched this play out like a made-for-TV movie series

a minor episode unfolded in Blount County Tennessee
fifteen black activists from Birmingham
fifteen white volunteers from the North
led by a white couple from Massachusetts by way of Vermont

North South Smoky Mountain Workcamp

the VW crawls around hairpin turns
groans up Old Cades Cove Road
on this farthest reach in Blount County
abutting the Smoky Mountain National Park

we hike a dirt path
push through brambles
stand in the meadow
partway up Rich Mountain
overlook Dry Valley
feel sunshine   feel breeze
this is our summer—
we're workcamp directors
we'll lead thirty volunteer campers
building a facility for interracial groups
for voter registration training

we enter a log cabin
one room and a loft
Bob kicks a rotten beam
wasps fly from under the eaves
field mice scramble into walls
I trace H-O-M-E in dust on a window

tomorrow: brooms
rags   trash-barrels

Tonight

we dream of
toilet paper
spring water
a stove and fridge
clean sheets and bed
a roof overhead

sweat-soaked   no chat
like Hansel and Gretel   we retrace steps
to our car   cross the road to the cabin
locate a rock labeled *Cadle*
rap on the door
no reply
Myles said we're expected
we unlatch the door
unroll sleeping bags
across gritty floor

Bob tunes his Mexican twelve-string
we sing *On Top of Old Smoky*
all covered with snow until
the kids' breath slows into sleep
Bob looks at me
I return his wary stare
fireflies spark by the window
cans rattle in the alcove—
Mr. Tillman Cadle is arriving

we're weary   fake sleep
feel Tillman hover
sense his shotgun over us
throughout the night
Tillman stumbles and mutters
there's going to be trouble

I *hope* he's *guarding* us
but I'm alert
ready to pick up the kids
ready to bolt

next I know   I feel sun
it's tomorrow
Tillman's asleep in a chair
shotgun on his shoulder
we tiptoe out

(decades later
I will learn Tillman Cadle
knew trouble when he smelled it
a retired Harlan County coal miner and organizer—
married to the folklorist Mary Elizabeth Barnicle
the recorder of Huddie Ledbetter and Aunt Molly Jackson—
Tillman offered the land for Highlander's use
he was the owner of record
he smelled trouble that night
he was right
we were his trouble
he   our guardian angel)

A Volunteer

is not some bleeding heart
do-gooder   good samaritan
but a down-to-earther
roll-up-your-sleever
ready to sign on
step up   chip in
pitch in   put to
put up   press
plunge tackle
hit on   gamble
adventurer

a volunteer is at the ready
a volunteer gets cracking

Workcamp Work

1
dawn ignites
one log cabin kitchen
thirty mouths to feed
from a secondhand refrigerator
four burners and an oven
I start coffee   boil grits
pack my kids into the bug
follow mountain roads to town
disregard glares and honks
shop for groceries and hardware
when the sun is high   back at camp
serve campers sandwich fixings

2
the women volunteers
from northern colleges
white women set on liberation
wear jeans and T-shirts
bandannas tied on hair
they steady planks and carry water
for men knocking tent platforms together
reeling electric cables to wire the kitchen
siphoning water through a hose
to jerry-rig a shower

3
the Birmingham women   movement workers
black women intent on equal rights and justice
settle for a cabin day in jammies
cooking up a storm of cornbread
laced with table scraps in a cast-iron skillet
frying chicken with a glaze of smoke
simmering collard greens with onions

on the side they keep
a beauty parlor running
heating straightening combs
applying Royal Crown Hairdressing
twisting strips of paper bags
setting hair in waving flips

at day's end they're ready
hair combed out and pretty
fresh pressed   a-swish and glowing
they call the sweaty workers
for a banquet of southern-style
home cooking

Crayola World

Robin draws sky-blue arches
burnt-orange sun   sepia earth sprouts
forest-green leaves
maroon father strums raw-umber guitar
bittersweet mother holds pink flower
purple sister sucks plum thumb

she leaves the center blank
surrounds the family
with smiling black people
dressed in magenta
teal-blue   lemon-yellow

she holds the white crayon
studies the empty space
studies her skin
why do they call me white?
I'm tannish-bananaish
puts down the crayon

I offer the peach labeled *flesh*
then hold up *tan*

she picks up *black*
draws herself in the center
that's me
the most beautifulest

A Visitor from Over Yonder

waves from the meadow *yoo-hoo*
I'm Florence come to help out
with the younguns a bit of a woman
in gingham armed with a hoe

friend or foe? reminds me of my granny
I holler *my kids could use some cultivating!*
she laughs *this thang's for copperheads!*
whomps the heads off a stand of daisies

Kristin rescues a blossom plucks its petals
Robin counts out *he loves me he loves me not*
Florence scoops up the girls *once upon a time*
Brer Fox tries to snag Brer Rabbit for a tasty treat …

a weathered man parks a beat-up truck
Florence calls out *yoo-hoo Sam over here!*
a crack of thunder a sudden downpour
thirty campers race through the cabin door

I offer Florence and Sam orange-crate seats—
I know some labor history I pinch myself
these neighbors are my heroes—
tell about Harlan County sing 'em your song!

Florence begins *in the thirties I was a mother*
with hardly a scrap of food for my younguns
Sam was a coal miner he stood up to the bosses
demanded fair wages spitfire lights her eyes

either you're with strikers or agin 'em
I tore a page from the calendar scribbled
some verses I made up on the spot to a hymn tune
marched out and joined that picket line

Florence sings out in a high mountain twang
will you be a lousy scab or will you be a man?
which side are you on?   which side are you on?
everyone listens rapt to her song   without

missing a beat   Birmingham campers
burst into the freedom song they march to
will you be an Uncle Tom or will you be a man?
which side are you on boys? which side are you on?

like Brer Rabbit and the Reeces   we're links
in a long skirmish to outwit Jim Crow
we sing out the stormy night
on the gutsy wings of song

The Sycamore Tree

draws us
under lacy shade
mottling our faces
the girls giggle

Robin traces the leaf veins
like Daddy's hands
gathers a swatch   swirls
I'm a bride! see my bouquet!
Kristin pats the flaking trunk
feel better soon, tree!

off-duty with my daughters
I soak in the scene—
the kids' mottled skin
like the camouflaged bark
the ants out on a limb
cutting chunks out of leaves

I see bleached bone
not a branch stripped of leaves

sycamore wood is for coffins

A Night Off

to a barbecue
hosted by a local chapter
of Congress of Racial Equality
in the backyard of a white family
in the city of scientific secrets—Oak Ridge

no one considers distance
no one considers mountain roads
no one considers breaking *local custom*—
young northern women (and men)
crammed for hours
in the backseats of dark cars
with young Birmingham men (and women)

Bob and Molly's fifth wedding anniversary—
they opt for a family evening at camp
just the four of them

2:30 a.m.

thirty campers return   some singing
black and white together   we shall not be moved
head to the surplus army tents

I hum along with the singing
it's Bob's night off
he's sleeping in the loft with our kids

I listen to the crickets
I do not hear cars pull up on the road
cut motors below the spring

I do not hear boots creep across turf
suddenly men in denim overalls
burst through darkness

I stand barefoot on the doorjamb
someone nudges me in the ribs with a gun
I don't budge   no one wears a badge

another sneers   *we're arresting you!*
I say words learned in civics class   *search warrant?*
someone jeers   *so you think you got rights?*

we're being swamped   surrounded
by a wall of white men pointing guns
crowding us   we are a herd

we're being rousted   my husband is shaking
we are the camp directors   they blame us
spit   *instigators*   shove us to head the line

march all thirty along the dirt road into night
my three-year-old grips my hand
my toddler raps on her daddy's chest

the intruders are raving
n_____ blood's gonna flow tonight
n_____ blood'll roll down this mighty mountain

a Birmingham voice sings *we are not afraid*
other campers join *we are not afraid tonight*
we drown out their rants with song

I am no longer shaking   I am singing
walking down a mountain with my family
in the middle of the night

Law Enforcement Officers (so called)

all white
some deputized that night
some members of the Ku Klux Klan
trespassed on private property
(abutting a national park boundary)
hid within sight of two tents and a cabin
hid within hearing of two tents and a cabin
no search warrant
no arrest warrant
no badges
no uniforms but denim
a so-called officer saw *black boys enter tent of white girls sit on beds*
a so-called officer saw *campers disrobing a girl unfastening a bra*
a so-called officer heard *campers giggling*
guns drawn officers advanced into camp
guns drawn officers ordered campers from tents
guns drawn officers ordered Mr. and Mrs. Gustafson and children from cabin
guns drawn said in unison *you're all arrested*
police rummaged found a pint of whiskey in a tent
police rummaged found a bottle of vodka in the cabin
police didn't say *threats received*
police didn't mention *into custody for protection*
police didn't allow extra diapers for the baby
police didn't allow flashlights
guns drawn police marched campers half a mile on the dirt path to the road
guns drawn police nudged campers into cars (later called *unmarked cruisers*)
guns drawn police placed *black boys* in car trunks
guns drawn police placed *a white boy* shouting *I insist on equal treatment* in a car trunk with black boys

transported all in a procession down mountain roads with switchbacks
    no outside threat visible   no vigilantes in sight
so-called arresters blared threats through intercoms at the campers all the
    way to Blount County Jail
guns drawn   officers of the law   marched thirty *suspects* inside   (*suspects*
    included the Gustafson children)
guns drawn   officers dispersed the group into holding tanks for drunks

In the Jailhouse

iron clanks iron   shuts out
starry sky   live oak trees   fireflies
even mosquitoes won't follow

my daughters and I are disappearing
into the sadness of stained mattresses
reeking toilet   no door   iron bars

I see the stranger   hair matted   mouth hard
circle   loom   ball her hands into fists
she demands   *in for drinking?*

I feel like a cockroach she must crush
I try finding   *that of God*   I think   *in her*
but something calms *my* breathing

three-year-old Robin pinches my hand
she's holding tight   I cling to magic
if she isn't crying   it isn't happening

shadows rim Robin's eyes   Kristin sobs
I haven't a hanky to wipe away tears
or fold into a puppet mouse to make them smile

what is a mother but a voice?
I open my mouth to improvise
to undo this night with song

any note will have to do
Robin matches my pitch
Kristin   don't   cry

we pick up pace   find song-shape
Kristin drones around her thumb
even the stranger rocks in rhythm

Kristin oh Kristin don't cry
Mummy is here   Robin is near
and Daddy is really close by

a guard peers through the bars
his raw hands pass me a paper bag
I press its hard cool   a bottle of milk!

the stranger shakes her head   *well I'll be*
at home the kids hate milk   I rip off the cap
they take turns swilling it down

like a mother cat
I use my spit to clean
their tear-streaked faces

this is how my mother cleaned me
how her mother cleaned her
we wrap the windless cell with song

Kristin oh Kristin don't cry
Mummy is here   Robin is near
and Daddy is really close by

Cellmate Betty Has Her Say

they don't care about you in here
alls they feed us
pig slop in a pie pan

now I got me a cigarette
I need a match   a damn match
for my damn cigarette

look at you—
bare knees
bare arms

you look like a kid
who are those
your kid sisters?

I got a kid
be two next month
they took my kid

jeez
stop gawking
at least my knees are covered

so the jeans are bloody
that's what you get
in a brawl

yup   been here three days
they call the grill owner
a bootlegger   call us *drunks*

yeah
I did some drinking
they arrested the lot of us

I'm the only lady
so here I am
in the lady slammer

can's got no door
no paper no flusher
just a head of overflowing crap

I gotta go
they won't give me a phone call
got no one to call

my old man's in here someplace
he'll lose his job
they gotta let him go

god   my head hurts
I'm taking these curlers out
they won't give me a comb

alls I got's what I's got on
I left my laundry in a paper sack
on the street   ruined by now

see that writing on the wall
God's my only help
but he ain't helping me

what kind of mother are you
bringing kids to jail?
you should be ashamed!

sing to those kids all you want
but jail-mummies
can't keep their babies

time sure drags in here

Captive

keys turn locks   gates clang open   clang shut   muffled moves   leather
shoes radio station rocks out the news   *communist training camp!*
thirty captured!

I flash back to being ten at the zoo   I watch the mama bear and cubs
eat and poop   the crowd whistles and hoots   I toss my red cape to
the sky   it flares   into the cage   the bears drag it to the den   crowd
taunts turn to screams   Daddy slaps me and slaps me—*I thought*
they'd got you!

now I'm the one behind bars with my kids   guards usher in Maryville
citizens   spiffed up   Sunday-best   this tidy mob wafts Evening in
Paris through the stench   they heckle   they mock us

the guard passes me a too-hot-to-touch tin can of coffee   it leaks   burns
my hands   spills over the floor   flows over bare toes   the mattress is
bare   knocked loose from the bunk   stained with grunge   the kids'
faces smudged   silky hair tangled   now we're the show

I'm an accused *agitator*   they describe me as *humble*   for the sake of the
kids I try for   *serene*   caught like the painted turtle the kids keep
in a basin   trapped like fireflies in the mason jar by their bed   I'm
red-baited   incarcerated   detained by deputies presumed KKK
overseen by the Grand Dragon of Tennessee   I   a white mother
can't protect my own kids   I'm humiliated   dominated   subjugated
in a kangaroo court

David Knows What to Do

herded into a cell with others
the door slams   he's locked in

an activist from Birmingham
his nineteenth arrest for rights

others rattle the cage bars
sing freedom the night through

he takes rest where he can
keeps strong for the long haul

moves into the corner
beds down on the floor

The Sheriff (when asked later)

claimed *I'd received phone calls*
claimed *they said goddamn n_____ blood'll run off that mountain*
claimed *they said you gotta do something*
claimed *we responded to alleged threats of violence*
claimed *my squad approached camp between 2:30 and 3 a.m.*
claimed *I am chief law enforcement officer of Blount County*
claimed *I had no choice I had to investigate*

Rev. Smith and Rev. Billups Drive Up from Birmingham

with bail money from Southern Christian Leadership Conference
these SCLC black clergymen have no time for fear
they take action—get all the kids out of jail
get the crew washed up   get 'em haircuts   get defense
scavenge clothes to dress modest   to look pressed
to look good in court   we're front-page news

while waiting for trial
all black and white campers
stay together in a church sanctuary
play guitar   sing *oh freedom over me*
graze from grocery bags at the parish table
sleep helter-skelter   on the floors   in the pews
play poker   smuggle in newspapers
sob over phone lines to parents

numb   I remember only feeling numb

Headlines

June 21st
Integrated Work Camp Raided
30 Held Pending Probe
Highlander Head Posts $4,500 Bond
Hearing for 8 in Raid Delayed
23 Arrested Not Charged
Obvious Persecution

June 22nd
Blount Jury to Probe Camp
District Attorney Sets Investigation

June 23rd
Blount Camp Closed
Hearings Set

June 24th
Fire of Mysterious Origins
Biracial Camp Destroyed
Log House, Tents Burned

June 25th
Blaze Destroys Biracial Camp
Camp Fire Called Arson
Right to Investigate Camp Upheld
2 Judges Hearing Raid Case
Case Continuance Denied

Blount County Presents Two Trials in One
(a legal farce in a two-day special-session)

SETTING:
a turn-of-the-century   steamy   packed-to-capacity   courtroom

CHARACTERS:
1 judge presides for the General Sessions Court
1 judge presides for the Juvenile Court
1 attorney for the state
1 attorney for the prosecution
1 attorney for the defendants
1 Oak Ridge scientist expert witness
2 camp directors   (27-year-old white man & 25-year-old wife)
5 workcampers   (2 black men   2 black women   1 white woman)
200 spectators   (overflow crowd loiters on lawn)
23 arrested   (not charged   barred from court   camp outside on the steps)
(the Gustafson daughters are not cast in this play)

PROSECUTION TESTIFIES:
disorderly conduct observed by police officers and sheriff
while protecting campers from bloodshed

GRAND DRAGON OF TENNESSEE'S KKK SHOUTS:
(from front-row wheelchair) amen!

DEFENSE TESTIFIES:
no search or arrest warrants shown   none issued
police officers left public roads and property
arrests on private property violate constitutional rights

STATE TESTIFIES:
officers never left the public road to observe campers   (in the dark   half a mile uphill to the tents   in the underbrush   surrounded by trees)

GRAND DRAGON OF TENNESSEE'S KKK SHOUTS:
(from front-row wheelchair) amen! amen!

POLICE AND SHERIFF TESTIFY:
black and white male and female campers in the same tent talking
one girl adjusting her bra

GRAND DRAGON OF TENNESSEE'S KKK SHOUTS:
(from front-row wheelchair) amen! amen! amen!

POLICE AND SHERIFF TESTIFY:
no physical contact seen

PROSECUTION ESTABLISHES:
Blount County is a dry county this trial is for liquor possession

DEFENSE TESTIFIES:
so-called vodka found in the cabin confiscated from a camper the bottle labeled *Vodka* contains only *water* (a tip-off from the stepfather of an underaged camper who'd lied about his age, the stepfather wanted to teach his kid a lesson when he opened it)

THE OAK RIDGE SCIENTIST AN EXPERT WITNESS IN FLUIDS:
not allowed to open the bottle
not allowed to testify
not allowed to question the contents of the bottle

Evidence against Mrs. Gustafson

1 *Nature, Man and Woman* by Alan Watts
a drawing of naked bodies on the cover
(her name inscribed left on her bedside)

2 audiotape of Bob Moses rallying support for Mississippi civil rights
(unlabeled left in the VW tape player)

3 cotton shift bought in a Maryville supermarket
(Mrs. Gustafson wore as a nightdress when taken at gunpoint to jail)
the defense lawyer wants to show it is modest
Mrs. Gustafson is 5′1″ the lawyer is 6′2″
he unrolls the dress
it falls to his belt
looks skimpy

courtroom erupts in guffaws

no mention is made of *a fire of mysterious origin*—
mysterious if empty kerosene cans don't count—
a fire that destroyed the work camp the evening before the trial
a fire that destroyed all personal belongings including
Mrs. Gustafson's in-process graduate school journals
notes and a draft of her thesis—
THE VOLUNTEER WORKCAMP: A TOOL FOR SOCIAL RECONSTRUCTION

Duet by Two Judges

swinging gavels—
guilty guilty   guilty

Mr. and Mrs. Gustafson
bound over to the Grand Jury

the rest of you
pay your fines
you are free to travel
out of Blount County
go today!

More Headlines

June 26th

Charges of Lewdness Dismissed Against 7
Six Guilty of Disorderly Conduct
Grand Jury Finds Camper Guilty of Lewdness—$15 Plus Costs
Camper & Director—Guilty of Possession of Alcohol: $10 Plus Costs
Directors Charged—Contributing to the Delinquency of Juveniles

June 27th

All Defendants to Appeal
Camp Directors Bound to Grand Jury
The Wrong Approach
Travesty of Justice

The Woman Cradles Her Children

she wants to hide from headlines
her white face no longer
slips through crowds incognito
her smile no longer smooths away hate
her manners can't undo
the smack of her Yankee accent
her heart hasn't cured any bigots

she'd worn motherhood like a shield
put her babies in harm's way
she's been spat on   jailed
tried in a kangaroo court
taunted by the KKK

she's weighted by wrongs
trapped in the snares of southern justice
shamed

Race Riff

in a race against time
she'd raced pell-mell for a cure
ignored questions on race
when pressed
filled in the blank for her kids
with *human*
her mind raced ahead
no more races to nowhere
she'd stumbled through brush
sought a safe haven
not raceways of racists
no more raiders screaming
n_____ blood's gonna flow
no more riots on newscasts
no more fire hoses on children
no more guns in her ribs
her heart racing   risky
not racy   like lovers
racy like losing it
was she losing it right here?
her white-looking youngsters
her husband part Mohawk
or was it Nipmuc?
bloodlines disappear
everyone passing
no time for quibbles
no time to work fractions
she must take hold
get into action

Phone Calls

from Bob's sister
we read the story in the New York Times

from the Haitian graduate student
how could you take your babies to jail

from the director of the graduate school
we'll make going to jail a condition for graduation   heh heh

from my brother
I can get you $25 to help out

from friends Pete and Toshi Seeger
we're mailing you a hundred bucks for research—
you kids will need it

Begging for Help

I call my parents in Woodstock   Connecticut
no answer

maybe my aunt in Kingsport   Tennessee?
she wears falsies
makes rum pies
hosts hubby's poker parties
she spoiled the kid me
but thinks politics
spoiled the adult me

I thumb yellow pages
churches
I can't embarrass my clergy father more

I dial the Society of Friends
someone answers   *how may I help thee?*

I think of my kids   I beg
can you help a family of four?
bound over to the grand jury
a trial   maybe next month
we're broke   no one left to call

the anonymous voice is even   is practical
I'll ask around for thee, friend
what's your home meeting?
I clear my throat   speak the truth
a Quaker high school   I add
sometimes we attend Cambridge Meeting

I wait   knowing I've asked strangers
for protection—one historic reason
for joining a Friends meeting   mutual protection
I resolve if I get through this rough mess
I'll join Cambridge Friends Meeting

the voice returns   *a couple in meeting*
two kids bunking at camp   thee may use
the boys' single rooms—
each room   a twin bed   two mats on the floor
stretch meals of pasta and rice

instant family
hot water
clean sheets
basic food
$125

we might make it through

Transparent

who knew?
a glass door
who saw?
always open

our hosts
away for the day
the first time since the raid
our family   together   alone

Bob pours morning coffee
strides toward the patio
glass shatters
shards slash his legs
gash his arms
cut his head
he crashes
hard to the floor
spurting blood—
I think he's dead

we'd driven south high
riding on wings of freedom
through invisible walls
we didn't hear cracking
we kept flying   kept smashing
through what we weren't seeing

the ER stitches
and bandages Bob
issues a press release
the story run on page one
retries the court case
of outside agitators—
of Bob's accident   a mere mention

at home in New England
our four parents
in consensus (for once)
working with commies!
busted with babies!

they let the phone ring

1963 SOUTH TO NORTH

Our Defense Lawyer

tall   talks with a drawl
a local guy   wife and kids
not looking for a fight
a lawyer who never blinked
when we asked him

he believes the law will do its work
he has no experience with law enforcers
making up testimony
not possible
not here
until
even he sees
the law is wearing blinders
he can't win
not this time
not in 1963
in Blount County Tennessee

his wife walks out taking the kids
friends and relatives shun him
clients drop from his practice
the bar association threatens disbarment
unless he departs Tennessee

he's broken   alone
sells his furniture
his home
flees the state of his birth

Sinking

our cash is gone
credit depleted
we're burned down like the cabin
broken up like the workcamp
gunned out like the car engine
charges hanging
more trials to come
master's degrees in question
we want to teach—
believe education the gateway—
will anyone hire us?

we're sinking   not sunk
like our car   battered and bruised
we get the engine fixed up
get it back on the highway
whizzing by pickups
trying to bump us off the road—
but no stopping this time
we drive straight to Putney

August at Putney Graduate School

we chug back up Putney Mountain
bake a heart-shaped birthday cake
slather it with pink frosting
adorn it with fresh strawberries
for Robin's fourth birthday

the Brattleboro Reformer
runs an in-depth story
Couple Plunged into Racial Horror
people we do not know reach out—
touching us is touching the Movement

but I can't pause   I can't care
time's up in three and a half weeks—
with or without master's degrees
we'll leave for destination unknown
on the day Kristin turns two

Appeal

shift a few letters
hear the peal of church bells
smell apple peels left from a pie

maybe a plea
a proposition
a seduction
a hustle
an angle
a lure

on August 6th
without razzle-dazzle
the district attorney moves
for dismissal of our petition
to the Tennessee Supreme Court
for a Writ of Error

he's refused our appeal

Two Days of Typing

Bob thumps his thumb
puffs cigarette after cigarette
pounds out a thesis
white man on a timetable—
look out White America
change is zooming down the tracks
charging right atcha

Bob hits the road
drives south solo—
he's an activist hero
when he shows up
at the Newport Folk Festival
he gets a standing ovation—
keeps on driving
joining thousands
marching for the vote
marching for jobs
marching for homes
marching for schools
marching on Washington
marching for freedom

I Panic in Putney

I'm mad at Sheriff Trotter
        he snagged my thesis
mad at Highlander
        Myles got me into this mess
mad at our lawyer
        he can't get me out of it
I'm mad at Bob   I'm really mad at Bob

I begin a new thesis
I have no idea what will come
I type   floodgates spew—

this shirtwaist wife
(that's me   in my pale blue dress
styled like a man's button-down)
this shirtwaist wife
catalogs a world in crisis—
Chinese starve
grain rots in Topeka
Haitian life expectancy: 29
conservationist   smeared as *communist*
birth control unavailable   untaught

I restate my original quest—
women seek meaning   (meaning me)
women can contribute solutions   (me again)
and nurture the next generation (amen)

I type my last words
as the kids peer into
the black and white TV
looking for the dot that is Daddy
in the crowd witnessing
Dr. King lifting the nation
with *I Have a Dream*

Happily Ever After All Over Again?

we retreat to Cambridge
the *Boston Traveler runs* a front-page story
Mom, Why Are We in Jail?

I'm astonished to see myself quoted
We tried to be nice to the men who took us to jail
They thought what they did was right

a rock smacks our apartment door
a note   tied on with string   *go back to Sweden*
where they sleep with n______s

Blinders Off

we take our new degrees in education and organizing
and interview at the American Friends Service Committee

Bob lands a job organizing on Blue Hill Avenue
with Jim Reeb (later Rev. Reeb will be martyred in Selma)

the AFSC asks me *how many words a minute do you type, honey?*
I will not be desperate I slam the door on secretarial work

news breaks of a bombing in 16th Street Baptist Church in Birmingham
killing Sunday school girls Cynthia Carole Denise and Addie May

despite indictments hovering over me I land
a teaching job in a cooperative in a Congregational church

I open the mail lift out a Massachusetts-issued
lifetime teaching certificate despite replying *yes* to *arrested?*

Cambridge Friends Meeting hires us to co-lead
weekend workcamps in Roxbury *of course take your kids!*

plus! a year of planning for a six-week summer workcamp
for international volunteers working on solutions in inner-city Roxbury

we've returned to live a few blocks from our old address
now wherever we look we see injustice—

hear rumors of public lynchings long ago near our street—
I wonder is this happily-ever-after?

November 22

the announcer on the car radio interrupts the music
Kennedy assassinated by sniper's bullets

Kristin and I are picking Robin up from school
parents hug each other   crying   hug their kids

at night   in bed   Robin needs to know
why did they shoot President Kennedy?

what can I say?   *he was a good man doing good*
I lean over   kiss her good night

she asks again   *he was doing good*
my daddy does good too—
          when will they kill Daddy?

Outside Agitator N____-Lover Commie (1964)

I'm training Boston volunteers
for Mississippi Freedom Summer
to use nonviolent resistance
in the face of threats and epithets
that will surely be hurled at them
I taunt them as I was taunted
not fun   this job pulls up hard memories—
one year since the raid and arrest
one year since our workcamp was razed
one year of shame and nightmares

news breaks *three civil rights workers*
missing in Mississippi   presumed slain—
Chaney   Goodman   Schwerner—
silence descends on the room
I see shock on sober faces
some weep
I can't think what to say
we take hands   form a circle
someone hums *we shall overcome*
we join in singing
yes   this time it was Mississippi
but we know it could be Tennessee
Connecticut   Vermont
or here in Massachusetts
it could be us   we sing softly in prayer
we are not afraid today
deep in my heart I do believe
singing carries us—
the next day all return

Instructions at Rev. Reeb's Home (1965)

no TV don't answer the phone
wait until their mother comes home

I've been tidying up supper dishes
starting bedtime routines

his kids peeking through curtains
my kids sleeping in Cambridge

flashing cruisers   TV crews   floodlights
nuns in habits   clergy in collars

some neighbors   some strangers
hold lighted candles   singing—

this little light of mine
I'm going to let it shine

I'm inside his home trying for normal
no one speaks   no one sings   all is still

the whole world knows
what his kids aren't told

no TV don't answer the phone
wait until their mother comes home

1963 Ends December 6, 1965

Blount County Criminal Court ordered
cases pending against defendants
nolle prosequi

meaning after paying court costs
neither side wins nor loses
both sides walk free

unofficial communication
due more to Alcoa Aluminum's recruiting needs
than to any civil rights guarantee

unofficial communication
your records will be wiped clean

unofficial communication
never return to Tennessee

unofficial communication
never write about this case

AFTER 1963

Jim Crow Lurks When

they say *he's uppity*
they say *that's very white of you*
they say *he's an oreo black outside white inside*
they say *she's a banana yellow outside white inside*
they say *I don't even think about race—*
they say *some of my best friends are—*
they say *but you don't even look—*
they say *I don't even think of you as—*
they say *I'm colorblind*

My Mother Says I'm Not Afraid Anymore (1984)

as she fastens gold hoops
into her newly pierced ears
pauses before sitting
at her birthday present
an Apple II computer
today she is seventy-five
no longer the young woman
in the Kentucky mountains
no longer cast as the minister's wife
she's retired from teaching English
a person with time to think
now she accepts her elder daughter's divorce—
and remarriage to an atheist Jewish teacher—
the way she accepts her younger daughter's
marriage to a Catholic Irish poet
she knows her sons-in-law   Dan and Ted
are blessings in her life
she accepts that women may love women
men may love men
she finds these changes interesting
even compelling   refreshing
even right

she leans close to me
I reckon you did right in 1963
in the civil rights movement
do you hear me?
I'm talking to you
I'm proud

Your People (2000)

my son-in-law says
call us Indians   call us Native Americans

whatever you say they're your people's names
for my people   we are Nipmuc

his six-year-old daughter—my granddaughter—asks
do you know what your people did to my people?

I remember learning long after my children had grown
some ancestors were Klansmen   some slaveholders

I admit   *a couple deported from a Scottish prison for being Presbyterians*
pushed against the Cherokee nation to settle in the Smoky Mountains

I add   *I am sorry they did that   and my people are your people*
she blurts back   *oh my god!*

Kinfolk (2005)

a voice I do not know on the phone
I was fixin to send y'all an invite
but here's a holler on the horn

the voice continues *I'm calling about*
the Dryden family gathering
I reply *my mother the only Dryden died*

if your mom's a Dryden you're one too
I want you to skedaddle on down
and be with us we're your folks

I'd never thought of myself as a Dryden
didn't know Mom had any kin but I turned lonesome
hearing Mom's voice in this cousin's speaking

I drive down the Blue Ridge Mountains
to an area forty miles from our workcamp site
share stories with newfound mountain kin

I stand in the Dryden log cabin built before towns
before state lines in good repair still lived in
my bloodline Presbyterian frontiersmen

once outsiders from Scotland they rooted here
same as the forebears of the folks on that raid
I could be they they me maybe we're cousins

I hear what my mom might say *dern tootin!*
that civil rights stuff was a rough mess for families
I'm glad y'all got started working it out

Civil Rights Update (2014)

the girl in skin-tight jeans
strains toward the mirror
mascaras her lashes
adjusts a third earring
plugs in an iPod
flounces off
in a wake
of attitude

she knows the story—
her grandmother
not much older than she
packed up two babies
drove dusty Tennessee roads
through drought-dry cotton fields
where tenant farmers
trying to register   trying to vote
were fired   were evicted
were harassed by the Klan

her grandmother
put her life on the line
went to jail with babies in tow

but sometimes she wonders
why didn't Grandma stay home?

she's serious about making a difference
studied the example of Dr. King
starred as Rosa Parks in the play
she's steeped in the language of rights
argues about curfew
posts hopes on Facebook
imagines herself a singer
doctor   engineer   poet
as if walking the aisles of T.J. Maxx
for a readymade fit off the rack
until bored   she tries on
a new way to make a difference

the girl   really a young woman
has not walked with the rhythmic feet of protest
is unaware of the care activists used in dressing
Brylcreemed hair   polished shoes   pressed shirts
clip-on neckties   the kind that unclip
when gripped   their eyes on the prize
picking-off big-picture fights — bus boycotts
freedom rides   lunch counter sit-ins
they marched for jobs   votes   schools
singing songs to freedom's beat

this girl owns her civil rights
but cannot imagine her vote counts
she does not know she is living the dream
but must keep dreaming it
or the movement will stop

Jim Crow still tramps the street

We Shall Overcome

we shall overcome
we shall overcome
we shall overcome some day
deep in my heart, I do believe
we shall overcome some day

we'll walk hand in hand
we'll walk hand in hand
we'll walk hand in hand some day
deep in my heart, I do believe
we shall overcome some day

we are not afraid
we are not afraid
we are not afraid today
deep in my heart, I do believe
we shall overcome some day

Traditional hymn, new words attributed to Zilphia Horton, Pete Seeger, and Guy Carawan at Highlander Center

ACKNOWLEDGMENTS

The day after the towers fell I quit my job and sat down to write this story. It took me a long time and was hard work. Fifty years had passed, and I still had nightmares. I chose to write it in poems to limit my discomfort as I chiseled and sifted one image at a time, building the story poem by poem.

Most of this story has not been documented or told previously. When I was hazy on the chronology and could not locate information, I have written what may have happened, what probably happened. I set down the truth as I know it and the facts as I located them, told through the eyes of a narrator named Molly, very like myself, but not exactly myself.

Over the past fifty years I have read hundreds, maybe thousands, of books and articles about the civil rights movement, the Appalachian mountain people, the peace movement, the women's movement, Quakerism, racism, experiential education and protest songs. This ongoing research forms the focus for my life and teaching. And I continue to sing as I work at home and when friends gather.

One article supported me in understanding the legal case as contained in existing records: "Raid on the Mountain: A 1963 Trial in Blount County Portrays the Turbulence of the Civil Rights Movement" by R. Culver Schmid, *Tennessee Bar Journal* (TBJ), volume 38, no. 1, January 2002. I read and reread the "Trial Transcript: State of Tennessee v. Robert L. Gustafson, et al."

My husband, Daniel Lynn Watt, and I returned to Tennessee in 2007. We attended the seventy-fifth anniversary celebration of Highlander, and talked with Sam Clark, a workcamp participant. We visited the site of the North South Smoky Mountain Workcamp in Blount County and with Viola McFerren in Fayette County. The librarians at the Nashville Public Library Civil Rights Room gave us access to a collection of photographs and newspaper clippings. The staff at the Benjamin L. Hooks Institute for Social Change at the University of Memphis gave access to their collection of Fayette County historical materials. I reread *Our Portion of Hell —Fayette County, Tennessee: An Oral History of the Struggle for Civil Rights* by Robert Hamburger (Links Books, 1973) to remind me of talking with John McFerren in 1963.

The poems in this volume make a story told in the company of each other. I have published a few as stand-alone poems, but they are much changed here. Some appear in my book *Shadow People* (Ibbetson Street

Press, 2007), in volumes of the *HILR Literary Review*, and in anthologies of *Bagels with the Bards*. An early version of "Civil Rights Update" is paired with Dr. Martin Luther King's "I Have a Dream" speech in the ninth-grade curriculum of the Dallas public schools. And it is posted on the website Bruce Hartford maintains, Veterans of the Civil Rights Movement. I read excerpts for the YouTube video *My Story: Molly Lynn Watt*, produced by the American Repertory Theater (ART) as a resource to a play it produced, *All the Way*, showing President Lyndon B. Johnson as midwife to the Civil Rights Act of 1964. The heart of my story is in an oral history conducted by Hailey Revie, Brooklynn Rucinski, and Alex Soukup, middle school students in D. C. Everest Area School, Wisconsin, and published in *The Nation's Longest Struggle: Looking Back at the Modern Civil Rights Movement* (2013).

I am deeply grateful to Martha Collins for support in shaping the manuscript.

I am grateful to Afaa Michael Weaver for support in starting the story.

I am grateful to the community of writers associated with the William Joiner Institute for the Study of War and Social Consequences at the University of Massachusetts Boston, where I found mentors and colleagues.

I am grateful to Suzanne Berger and to members of her Advanced Poetry Writing Workshop at Lesley University and Fran Vaughan and the members of the poetry workshops at HILR at Harvard University.

I am grateful to Marilyn Nelson for a writing residency at Soul Mountain in East Haddam, Connecticut, and Joyce Maynard for a writing residency at Lake Atitlán in Antigua, Guatemala.

I am grateful for feedback from the faithful at the Fireside Readings, the Bagel Bards of Somerville, and Artists and Writers of Cambridge Friends Meeting.

I am grateful to the Divers Writing Group (Jean Alonso, Susan Freireich, Bette Steinmueller, Linda Stern, and Nancy Teel), and the Thursday Project (Bernadette Davidson, Holly Guran, Debbie Pfeiffer, Ruby Poltorak, Elizabeth Quinlan, and Barbara Thomas).

I give a special thank you to Kate Frank, Florence Ladd, Fred Marchant and Julie Rochlin, for listening with a generous ear many times.

I am grateful to Myles Horton for the honor of working at Highlander. I am grateful to Pam McMichael, the current director of Highlander, for commenting on an early draft. I am grateful to Thorsten Horton and Sam Clark, who proposed the workcamp initially, and led the construction work.

I am grateful to Morris Mitchell, the director of the Putney Graduate School of Teacher Education, now the Antioch/New England Graduate School, for the privilege of traveling with him.

I am grateful to Doug Holder of Ibbetson Street Press, for publishing *On Wings of Song*; to Steve Glines for designing it; to Ruth Goring for copy edits and to Bridget K. Galway for her painting, *Good Company*, on the cover. It reminds me of my young self reaching from Putney Mountain to Rich Mountain, yearning for more.

I am grateful to my first husband, Robert Lincoln Gustafson, for taking this journey with me and our daughters, Robin Chase Gustafson and Kristin Lynn Gustafson. When Dr. Martin Luther King was assassinated, our marriage, like the nonviolent movement, floundered and Bob and I took different paths of conscience.

I am grateful to my grandchildren, Moira, Brian, Lydia, Keely, and Alice, who asked, "Why did you take Mummy to jail?"

I am grateful to my husband, Daniel Lynn Watt, for living the writing sojourn with me. He, a participant in the Fayette County voter registration project in 1964, believes as I do, when citizens participate together, *we shall overcome*.

Molly Lynn Watt, Cambridge, Massachusetts, 2014

A NOTE ABOUT THE AUTHOR

photo by Phillip McAlary

Molly Lynn Watt, poet, activist and educator, worked at Highlander Center in Tennessee in 1963. She pursued a professional life committed to leading educational reform and experiential learning with diverse communities of learners from three months of age to learners well into their nineties. She was a cofounder of the Folksong Society of Greater Boston, Teacher Center Brookline, the Action Research Center at EDC and the Logo Institute. She served on the Martin Luther King Speakers Bureau. Her book of poems, *Shadow People,* was published by Ibbetson Street Press in 2007. She served as editor of *Bagels with the Bards Anthology,* volumes 1-4, as poetry editor for the *HILR Review*, and curator of the Fireside Readings. She and her husband, Daniel Lynn Watt, coauthored and perform *George and Ruth: Songs and Letters of the Spanish Civil War*, also available from CD-Baby. They are cofounders of Cambridge Co-housing in Massachusetts, where they live and play in the Uncommon Strummers Ukulele Band.